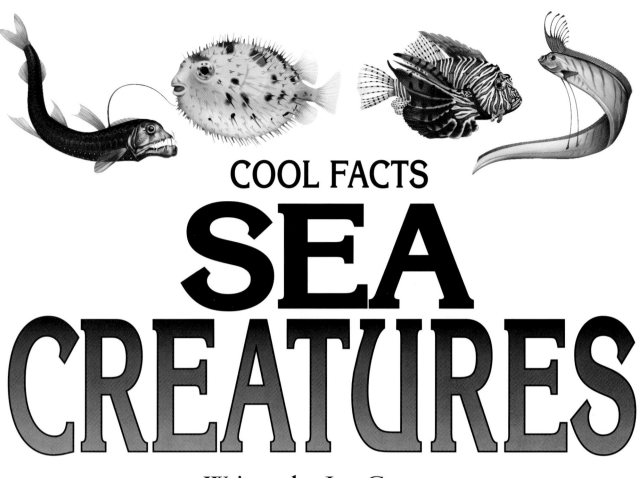

COOL FACTS
SEA
CREATURES

Written by Jen Green
Illustrated by Michael Posen

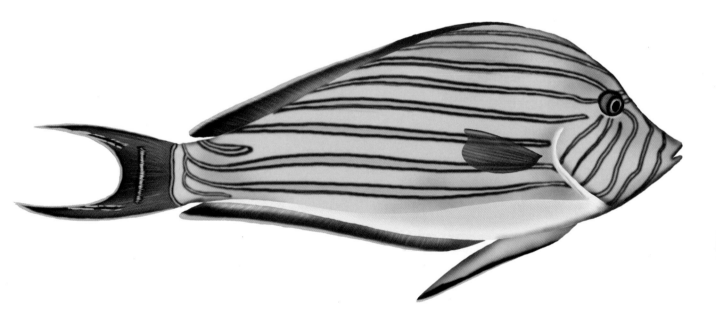

This is a Parragon Book
This edition published in 2001

Parragon
Queen Street House
4 Queen Street
Bath BA1 1HE, UK

ISBN 0-75255-049-7

Printed in Dubai, U.A.E

Produced by
Monkey Puzzle Media Ltd
Gissing's Farm
Fressingfield
Suffolk IP21 5SH
UK

Cover design: David West Children's Books

Contents

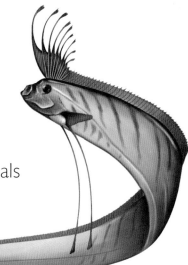

Why do most fish have slim, tapering bodies?

MOST CREATURES THAT SPEND THEIR WHOLE LIVES IN WATER HAVE A

sleek, streamlined shape that helps them to swim. Fish come in many different shapes and sizes. Eels are long and slender, plaice and rays are flat. Angelfish are tall and thin, so they are hard to see from the front as they approach their prey. Other fish are rounded, but almost all have a tapering shape that allows them to slip easily through the water.

Oarfish

Which is the world's longest fish?

Oarfish are giant, eel-shaped fish that regularly grow over 6 m (20 feet) long. Individuals as large as 14 m (46 feet) long have been recorded. Legends of sea serpents may have been inspired by glimpses of these amazing creatures.

The oarfish's ribbon-like shape helps it to glide through the water.

Which is the tallest fish?

Ocean sunfish are tall fish that can measure over 4 m (14 feet) high, including their long back and belly fins. These large fish can weigh over 2 tonnes.

Why are flatfish flat?

Flatfish such as plaice, halibut and dab live on the sea-bed. Their flattened shape allows them to glide along the bottom, and to lurk on the sea floor, lying in wait for animals to eat.

How do fish hide in the open sea?

Herring, mackerel and many other fish that swim near the surface of the great oceans have dark backs and pale bellies. This colouring, called countershading, works to cancel out the effect of sunlight shining on their bodies from above, and so helps these fish to hide even in open water.

What creatures plant a garden on their backs?

Spider crabs make their own disguises from materials they find in the sea around them. They clip living sponges or fronds of seaweed with their strong pincers, and plant them on their backs. When the seaweed dies, they replace it with a fresh piece!

Why do some fish have bright colours?

Many fish that live in tropical seas are brightly coloured or marked with bold spots and patterns. This colouring helps them to hide among the brightly coloured coral and dark shadows, but also helps them to stand out clearly in open water. In the breeding season, when these fish are seeking mates and want to be noticed, they swim out into the open and become very obvious.

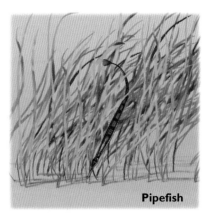

Pipefish

Predators find it very difficult to spot pipefish hiding among strands of seaweed.

What fish looks like seaweed?

Pipefish are long, slim, dark green fish that look just like strands of seaweed. In shallow, weedy waters, they swim upright among the seaweed fronds, and resemble their surroundings so closely that they are almost impossible to see.

Carpet shark

The carpet shark's camouflage helps to conceal it from its prey.

How does the carpet shark stay hidden?

MANY SEA CREATURES HAVE BODIES WITH COLOURS, shapes and patterns that blend in with their surroundings. This natural disguise, or camouflage, helps them to hide from enemies or sneak up on their prey. Carpet sharks live and hunt on the sea-bed. Their pale, blotchy colours help hide them from their prey – small fish and crabs – as they lie motionless on the bottom.

5

Flying fish leap up to 2 m (6 feet) in the air, and glide along with outstretched fins.

What sea creature looks like a pair of false teeth?
Scallops have a hard, hinged shell to protect their soft bodies. Some kinds of scallop swim along by clapping the two halves of their shell together so water shoots out of the back. The swimming scallop looks like a pair of false teeth chattering as it zips along!

Which fish is the fastest swimmer?
Sailfish are large hunting fish that live in the open ocean. With their long, streamlined snouts, torpedo-shaped bodies and powerful tails, they can speed along at up to 109 kph (67 mph).

Which sea creature is the deepest diver?
Sperm whales are expert divers. Like all whales, they breathe at the surface, but swim down to depths of 500 m (1,600 feet) to hunt deep-sea creatures such as giant squid. The snouts of sperm whales often bear the scars of battles with the squid.

Which fish flies through the air?
FLYING FISH TAKE TO THE AIR TO ESCAPE FROM HUNGRY PREDATORS SUCH as sailfish and marlins. The flying fish gets up speed, then leaps right out of the water. In the air, it spreads its chest fins so they act like wings, keeping the fish airborne for up to 100 m (325 feet).

How do fish swim?
Most fish swim by arching their bodies and swishing their tails from side to side. The fish's body and tail push against the water to propel it forwards. The chest, back and belly fins help with steering and braking. A gas-filled organ called the swim bladder keeps the fish buoyant in the water.

Which sea creature uses jet-propulsion?
The octopus has a funnel-shaped siphon sticking out from its body. It shoots a jet of water from the funnel to propel itself along, and can point its siphon in different directions to steer.

Which fish "flies" underwater?
Rays are flattened fish that live near the sea-bed. They swim along by flapping their wide, flat chest fins like wings, so they look as if they are flying underwater.

Mudskippers survive on land by filling their large gill-chambers with water.

How do jellyfish get about?
Jellyfish are soft creatures with bodies shaped like bells or saucers. To get about, they contract their bag-like bodies so water shoots out behind, pushing the creature along.

Which fish can walk on land?
Mudskippers are fish that live in swamps and muddy estuaries on tropical coasts. They come right out of the water and scurry about on land, using their muscular chest fins as crutches.

Mudskipper

Why do dolphins leap out of the water?

DOLPHINS AND WHALES HAVE TAILS THAT ARE FLATTENED HORIZONTALLY, not vertically like fish-tails. They swim by sweeping their tails up and down. When swimming at speed, dolphins leap out of the water to save energy, because is is quicker and easier to move through air than water. Like all water-dwelling mammals, dolphins must also surface to breathe.

How do barracuda surprise their prey?

The barracuda is a fierce hunting fish of tropical seas. It has keen eyesight and is armed with razor-sharp teeth. Its blue-grey colouring blends in well with the ocean, allowing it to sneak up on a shoal of small fish. The hunter speeds into the middle of the shoal with its jaws snapping, and seizes its prey in its deadly teeth.

How does the anemone catch its dinner?

Sea anemones are armed with a crown of stinging tentacles. When small fish brush against them, the stings fire and release a paralysing poison. Then the tentacles push the weakened prey into the anemone's mouth.

Which fish has a fishing rod?

THE ANGLERFISH HAS A BUILT-IN FISHING ROD ON ITS HEAD – A LONG, THIN spine with a fleshy lobe on the end that looks like a wiggling worm. The angler lurks on the sea-bed, squat-bodied and well-camouflaged. When a small crab comes up to eat the "worm", the anglerfish lunges forward and grabs its prey in its enormous mouth.

Which fish has a secret weapon?

The torpedo ray. It can generate electricity using special muscles in its head. The ray lurks on the sea-bed, waiting for small fish to pounce on. It wraps its fins around its victims and blasts them with a charge of 200 volts.

The anglerfish lures its prey with its built-in fishing rod, complete with bait.

Archerfish

Which fish runs a cleaning service?

SMALL FISH CALLED CLEANER WRASSE
feed on parasites that infest larger
fish. The big fish welcome this
cleaning service, so do not harm the
wrasse, even when it swims right inside a
big fish's mouth to clean. Sometimes queues of
fish form at the wrasse's cleaning station, patiently waiting
their turn for a "wash and brush-up".

Which fish shoots to kill?
On tropical sea coasts, skilled
archerfish can catch prey such as
spiders that are perched on plants
overhanging the water. With their
powerful lips, they squirt a jet of
water at their target and knock
their prey into the water.

Anglerfish

How do parrotfish eat their meals?
Parrotfish have hard mouths shaped like parrots' beaks.
With their tough mouths they scrape algae and coral
from the rocks. This food is then ground to a powder
by horny plates inside the
fish's mouth.

What fish is a thirsty bloodsucker?
Lampreys are strange fish with eel-shaped bodies.
Instead of jaws, they have round mouths filled with rows
of horny teeth. The lamprey uses its mouth as a sucker to
fasten on to another fish's body. Its teeth scrape away the
fish's skin, then the lamprey drinks
its blood!

What creature gives a nasty nip?

CRABS AND THEIR RELATIVES, LOBSTERS, BELONG TO A GROUP OF

shelled creatures called crustaceans. The crab's soft body parts are protected by a hard outer case that forms a snug suit of armour. The creature is also armed with powerful claws that can give a nasty nip if an enemy comes too close.

How do herring avoid being eaten?

Fish such as herring and mackerel swim in groups called shoals. Living in a large group provides safety in numbers, because it is difficult for predators to single out a likely target among a shifting, shimmering mass of fish.

What is slimy and hides in anemones?

In tropical seas, clownfish hide from their enemies among the stinging tentacles of sea anemones. The tentacles do not harm the clownfish because its body is covered with a thick layer of slimy mucus, but no predator dares to come close!

The hermit crab makes its home inside an abandoned sea shell.

Hermit crab

Which fish makes eyes at its enemies?

The twinspot wrasse has two dark patches on its back. Hunting fish may mistake the spots for the eyes of a large and possibly dangerous creature, and swim away. If this trick fails, the wrasse has another. It dives down to the sea-bed and quickly buries itself in the sand.

Why does the hermit crab need a home?

Unlike other crabs, the hermit crab has no hard case to protect it. Instead, it shelters its soft rear end inside an empty sea shell. As the crab grows bigger, its shell becomes too tight, so it moves into a larger new home.

Few predators will tackle a
porcupine fish once it has
inflated itself into
a spiny ball.

**Which creature can grow
four new arms?**
The starfish is a five-limbed sea
creature. If a hungry predator bites
off one of its arms, the starfish
can grow a new one to
replace it. In fact, it can
replace up to four of its
arms, provided the
central body of the
animal is unharmed.

Which fish blows itself up into a prickly ball?

The porcupine fish is named for the sharp spines, like a porcupine's,

that cover its body. Usually the spines lie flat against the fish's
body, but if danger threatens, it can raise them. If an enemy
comes too close, the fish takes in water so that its body
swells to twice its normal size. It becomes a prickly ball too
large and uncomfortable for predators to swallow. When
the danger passes, the porcupine slowly returns
to its normal shape and size.

**Which creature throws
ink at its enemies?**
Cuttlefish are relatives of squid
and octopus. Like their cousins,
they can produce a cloud of ink to
confuse their enemies. The
cuttlefish jets away under cover of
this "smokescreen".

**What makes a pistol shrimp
go bang?**
Pistol shrimps are named after the
cracking noise they make by
snapping their claws. Enemies are
frightened off by these unexpected
"pistol shots".

Spiny lobsters cover up to 15 km (9 miles) a day as they migrate along the sea-bed in a line.

Spiny lobsters

What buries itself in the sand?

MANY CREATURES THAT DWELL ON THE OCEAN BOTTOM ESCAPE

from their enemies by burying themselves in the sand or mud. Crabs dig down and lie low with just their sensitive antennae showing. Weeverfish, which hide in the same way, have eyes on top of their heads. Their eyes stick out above the sand so the fish can still see while the rest of its body is buried.

Which fish "walks" on three legs?

The tripod fish is a strange fish that lives in deep, dark waters. Its two chest fins and tail fin have long, stiff spines. Together, the three spines form a tripod which the fish uses to rest and move along the sea-bed.

The tripod fish uses its stiff spines like stilts to walk along the sea-bed.

Tripod fish

How did the butterfish get its name?

Butterfish are long, slender fish that live in pools on rocky sea-shores. The slimy, slippery feel of their bodies has earned them their name.

How does a limpet grip its rock?

The limpet clamps its muscular foot on to a seaside rock and grips by suction. Even the pounding waves cannot dislodge it. Its hold is so tight it can be prised away only if an enemy attacks without warning.

Which creature has five sets of jaws?

Underneath its round, spiny body, the sea urchin has a mouth with five sets of jaws. It feeds by crawling along the sea floor, scraping seaweed and tiny creatures from the rocks.

Why do crabs walk sideways?

All crabs have ten legs – eight for walking and two with powerful pincers for picking up food. Crabs scuttle sideways along the shore and sea-bed. The sideways movement helps to prevent them tripping over their own legs! Large species of crab move only slowly, but small ghost crabs can scurry along the shore at a fast clip.

What queues up for its winter holiday?

SPINY LOBSTERS LIVE MAINLY SOLITARY LIVES. BUT EACH YEAR IN autumn they gather to move to deeper waters where they will be safe from violent storms. The lobsters form a long line and march off along the sea-bed. When they reach their winter holiday destination they separate, and only meet up again to begin the long trip back.

Which fish would disappear on a chess board?

Plaice are flatfish that live on the sea-bed. In a matter of minutes, they can change their body colour from pale and sandy to dark or blotchy, to match their surroundings as they drift over the sea-bed in search of food. They can even adjust their colouring to become checkered if a chess board is placed under them! Only the upper part of the fish, visible to enemies, is coloured. The underside is white.

What needs a new suit of armour every year?

A crab's shell gives good protection. The disadvantage is that there is no space inside for the crab to grow! Each year, the crab sheds its old, tight skin and grows a new, slightly larger one. While the new soft skin is still hardening the creature is very easy to attack, so it hides away from enemies under rocks.

What is coral made of?

CORAL REEFS ARE MADE BY TINY CREATURES CALLED POLYPS

that live in colonies in tropical seas. Polyps are shaped like little sea anemones, but have a hard, chalky cup-shaped shell to protect their bodies. When they die, the shells remain, and new polyps grow on top of them. Over time, billions of shells build up to form a coral reef.

Surgeonfish

Where is the world's biggest coral reef?
The Great Barrier Reef off the north-east coast of Australia is the world's largest coral reef. Stretching for 2,000 km (1,200 miles), it is the largest structure made by living creatures. The reef is home to many spectacular animals, including 1,500 different kinds of fish.

What are dead man's fingers?
Dead man's fingers is a species of soft coral that grows on rocks. Each coral colony is made up of thousands of polyps that form a fleshy mass like a rubbery hand. When a piece of this coral washes up on the sea-shore, it may give swimmers a fright!

Why does a crown-of-thorns threaten coral reefs?
The crown-of-thorns starfish is a reef-killer. It fastens on to the living coral, sticks its stomach out, and releases juices that digest the coral polyps. When only the coral shells are left, the starfish moves on. It can kill a big patch of coral in a day, and has destroyed large areas of the Great Barrier Reef.

Leafy seadragon

Which fish has the head of a horse and the tail of a monkey?
The sea-horse is an unusual fish with a head shaped like the knight in a chess set. It holds its body upright and swims along by waving its back fins. It uses its long, curling tail to anchor itself in the seaweed while it searches for small creatures to eat. Its eyes can swivel independently, so the sea-horse can hunt for food and watch out for enemies at the same time!

The surgeonfish defends itself by lashing its tail, which is armed with razor-sharp blades.

Which fish can attack with a scalpel?
Surgeonfish of tropical seas have sharp little blades like scalpels at the base of their tails. Usually the bony blades lie flat against the fish's body, but they can be flicked out like knives if an enemy approaches.

What is a leafy seadragon?

THE LEAFY SEADRAGON IS A LARGE SEA-HORSE THAT LIVES IN warm Australian water. This creature is a master of disguise. Its body is covered with long, trailing flaps of skin that look like strands of seaweed. It is very difficult to spot as it swims among the weeds.

What clams up in a hurry?
Giant clams live on the Great Barrier Reef. Their huge, hinged shells measure up to 1.5 m (5 feet) wide, and weigh 250 kg (550 lb). The giant clam generally has its shell open so it can feed, but if danger threatens, it can slam the two halves shut. Inquisitive sea creatures had better watch out!

Ragged flaps of skin disguise the leafy seadragon as it drifts among the seaweed.

Hatchetfish

How do fish hide in dark seas?

Deep-sea fish are camouflaged to blend in with their surroundings. Many have black or dark bodies to match the inky waters. Others are transparent. Hatchetfish have silvery bodies that reflect any small gleams of light.

The hatchetfish has a line of tiny lights running down its belly that hides its shadow in the water.

What creatures can survive at great ocean depths?

A CENTURY AGO, SCIENTISTS BELIEVED THAT NO LIFE COULD EXIST in the very deep oceans. Now we know that creatures do survive there, but conditions are very harsh. A thousand metres (3,330 feet) below the sunlit surface, the water is pitch-black and very cold. Deep-sea fish must be able to stand the great pressure caused by the weight of water on top of them, which would kill surface creatures. Many deep-sea fish look like monsters from a horror film, with large heads, huge mouths with fierce teeth, and long, thin bodies. Yet most of these deep-sea horrors are very small – less than 30 cm (1 ft) long.

Viperfish

Why are deep-sea fish mysterious?

Scientists still know very little about deep-sea fish, because

of the difficulties of descending to the ocean bottom to study them. Most deep-sea fish don't survive if they are brought to the surface. Some even explode, because their bodies are built to withstand the great pressure of the ocean depths!

How do deep-sea creatures find their food in the dark?
In the black depths, many deep-sea fish sense their prey by smell, taste and touch. A line of nerves running down the fish's body picks up vibrations in the water caused by other swimming creatures. Some deep-sea hunters have long touch- and taste-sensitive tentacles trailing from their jaws.

Can deep-sea fish see in the dark?
For many deep-sea fish, vision is little use in the inky darkness. They have tiny eyes, or no eyes at all, and cannot see. Other fish have large eyes that pick up any faint glimmers of light, or tube-shaped eyes that work like binoculars. Still other species make their own light to hunt their prey.

Why don't gulper eels get hungry?
Food is scarce in the ocean depths, for no water plants and few creatures live there. So fishes' meals are few and far between. Gulper eels and viperfish have large, stretchy stomachs that can expand to fit any victim that passes. Another deep-sea fish, the black swallower, can swallow and digest a fish twice its own size.

With its giant mouth, the viperfish is a fierce deep-ocean predator. The long teeth point backwards to make sure no prey escapes from its jaws.

What hunts with a luminous "worm"?
Like other anglerfish, the deep-sea angler has a long, thin spine that forms a "fishing rod" to catch prey creatures. On the end of the spine, a luminous lure dangles like a glowing worm to attract the fish's victims.

How do deep-sea creatures light up the dark?
As many as 1,000 different fish make light in the deep oceans. Some have luminous bacteria living under their skin. Others have special light-producing organs, or can cause a chemical reaction that gives off light.

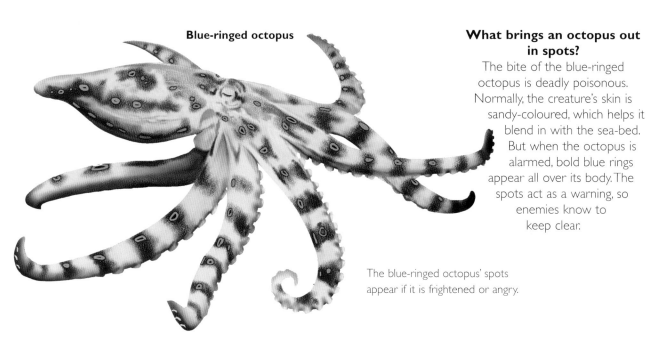

Blue-ringed octopus

What brings an octopus out in spots?

The bite of the blue-ringed octopus is deadly poisonous. Normally, the creature's skin is sandy-coloured, which helps it blend in with the sea-bed. But when the octopus is alarmed, bold blue rings appear all over its body. The spots act as a warning, so enemies know to keep clear.

The blue-ringed octopus' spots appear if it is frightened or angry.

How does a jellyfish sting?

The long, trailing tentacles of jellyfish are armed with thousands of tiny stinging cells. Some cells contain tightly-coiled barbs. When a careless fish brushes against a tentacle, the barbs fire to pierce the victim's skin and release a paralyzing poison.

Lionfish

Which is the world's most poisonous reptile?

The bite of the yellow-bellied sea snake is 50 times more powerful than that of the dreaded king cobra. Its bold yellow-and-black colours warn of danger.

Why are lionfish brightly striped?

THE LIONFISH IS A BEAUTIFUL BUT deadly fish of tropical waters. Its long, graceful spines contain a lethal poison. The lionfish drifts lazily though the water with its orange-striped colouring, yet few enemies dare to approach it. The fish's bright colours warn that it is poisonous. They are a signal known and recognized throughout the animal world.

What "stone" can kill you if you tread on it?

OVER 50 DIFFERENT KINDS OF POISONOUS FISH LURK IN THE WORLD'S OCEANS. Some are armed with venomous spines, others have poisonous flesh. The stonefish of Australian waters is one of the deadliest of all sea creatures. If a person treads on the fish, its spines release a toxin (poison) that causes agonizing pain. Numbness spreads through the victim's body, and they may die of shock, heart failure or breathing problems.

In Australian waters, the scary sea wasp jellyfish is responsible for more deaths than sharks.

The lionfish's striped colours warn enemies to keep well away.

What sea creature can sting a person to death in four minutes?

Jellyfish look fragile, but many species are armed with painful stings. The box jellyfish of Southeast Asia is so venomous that its sting can kill a person in just four minutes. The small sea wasp jellyfish of Australia is said to have the world's most painful sting.

Which deadly fish looks like a toad?

The toadfish is a poisonous fish that dwells on the sea-bed in warm oceans. The spines on its back fins and gill covers contain a strong venom that can cause great pain. With its bulging eyes, large mouth and blotchy skin, the fish is well-named, for it looks just like a toad.

Which poisonous fish do people eat?

The entrails of the pufferfish contain a powerful poison. Yet other parts of the fish are said to taste delicious! In Japan, the fish is served as a delicacy called fugu. Japanese chefs are trained to remove all traces of the poisonous organs, yet each year people die from eating fugu that has not been properly prepared.

What is the stingray's secret weapon?

Stingrays live and hunt on the ocean bottom. Their long, thin tails are armed with barbs that can inject a painful poison.

Estuarine crocodile

Which marine reptile is the biggest?

The saltwater crocodile is the world's largest sea-going reptile. This fierce giant grows up to 8 m (26 feet) long, and its jaws and teeth are jumbo-sized to match!

Saltwater or estuarine crocodiles are found on eastern sea coasts from India to Australia.

What sea creature is as big as four dinosaurs?

Speedy orcas grow up to 9 m (30 feet) long and weigh over 6 tonnes.

THE BLUE WHALE IS THE GIANT OF THE OCEANS. INDEED, IT IS the largest animal ever to have lived on Earth – four times the size of the biggest dinosaur! An adult blue whale measures up to 32 m (100 feet) long, and may weigh over 200 tonnes – as much as 60 elephants. Female blue whales are the biggest – the males are smaller.

What is the smallest fish?

The dwarf goby holds the record for the world's smallest fish. Adult dwarf gobies measure only 1 cm (0.4 in) long – about the width of your little finger. These tiny fish are found in the Indian Ocean.

What is the world's biggest crab?

The Japanese spider crab is the giant of the crab world. Its body measures more than 30 cm (1 ft) across, and a rowing boat would easily fit between its outstretched claws, which grow up to an astonishing span of 3.5 m (11 feet). At the other end of the scale, the tiniest crab is smaller than a pea.

What record-breaking fish came back to life?

Coelacanths are giant primitive fish that scientists knew from fossils, but believed had died out millions of years ago. Then in 1938, a living specimen of the "extinct" species was caught off South Africa. Now scientists in submersibles have studied coelacanths living on the sea-bed off the island of Madagascar. Coelacanths are giant, blue-scaled fish with muscly fins which they may use to perch on the ocean bottom.

Killer whale

What is the world's largest mollusc?

MOLLUSCS ARE A FAMILY OF SHELLED CREATURES THAT INCLUDE SLUGS, snails, clams, and also squid and octopus. The largest mollusc is the giant squid. These creatures commonly grow 3.6 m (12 feet) long, but specimens as large as 21 m (69 feet) have been found washed up on beaches. Scientists know little about these mysterious deep-sea creatures, which have never been seen swimming in the ocean depths.

What is the biggest fish?

Fish vary more in size than any other group of animals with backbones (vertebrates). The largest fish is the whale shark, which grows up to 15 m (49 feet) long and weighs 20 tonnes. Though giant in size, whale sharks are not fierce hunters. They feed mainly on tiny shrimp-like creatures called krill.

What are the tiniest sea creatures?

Thousands of kinds of tiny creatures live in the world's oceans. The smallest are made up of just one cell, and must be magnified a thousand times or more before we can see them. Plankton is the name given to the billions of tiny plants and animals that float near the surface of the oceans. They are the main food of many fish and other sea creatures.

Which is the fastest marine mammal?

The orca, or killer whale, is the speed champion among sea creatures. It can race along at up to 56 kph (34 mph) to overtake its prey.

What is a chimera?

According to Greek legend, the Chimera was a terrible

monster with a lion's head, a goat's body and a dragon's tail. Strange deep-sea fish called chimeras also look as if their bodies have been assembled from the parts of other creatures. They have large heads with staring eyes like bushbabies, and buck teeth like rabbits. Their bodies end in long, thin tails like rats' tails.

What is a kraken?

In olden days, myths and legends about dangerous sea creatures reflected the perils of ocean travel. Norwegian legends told of the kraken, a giant, many-armed monster that rose from the depths, wrapped its tentacles around unlucky ships and dragged them down to the bottom. This legend is thought to be based on sightings of the mysterious deep-sea squid.

What is a mermaid's purse?

Dogfish are small sharks. The tough case in which a baby dogfish develops is called a mermaid's purse. Sometimes the empty cases are found washed up on beaches, but it is unlikely that mermaids keep their treasures there!

Which fish has devil's horns?

The manta ray or devilfish has two fins that curve forward from its head like devil's horns. The ray uses its "horns" to scoop food into its mouth as it swims along the sea-bed.

Are there sea monsters in Massachusetts?

Early American settlers lived in fear of a huge sea serpent that was said to live off the coast of Gloucester, Massachusetts. The monster was supposed to have been scaly with a long tongue, but nobody really knows what it looked like – or if it even existed!

Manta ray

Which white whale ate Captain Ahab's leg?

Herman Melville's classic novel, *Moby Dick*, tell the story of Captain Ahab and his hunt for the great white sperm whale that tore off his leg. In his ship, the *Pequod*, Ahab and his sailors sail all around the world in search of the whale. When they finally catch up with Moby Dick, they struggle for three days to catch him. Ahab finally harpoons the great monster just as the whale sinks the ship, and the unfortunate captain is dragged down to a watery grave.

Which nymph ate sailors?

An ancient Greek legend tells of a beautiful nymph, called Scylla, who argued with the Gods and was turned into a terrifying monster by them. This horrific creature was said to have six heads, each with three rows of teeth. It lived in a sea cave, but would venture out of the deep to prey on creatures like dolphins, sharks and even sailors!

Who survived being eaten by a whale?

According to the Bible's Old Testament, a man called Jonah was travelling by sea when a storm blew up. Superstitious sailors cast the unlucky traveller overboard. A whale swallowed Jonah, but spat him out unharmed three days later. In reality, no one could survive in a whale's stomach for three days, because there would be no air to breathe.

The giant manta ray looks scary, but is generally harmless to humans.

What fish carries the "sword of the sea"?

The killer whale has a tall, thin back fin 2 m (6.5 feet) long, that sticks straight out of the water like a sword. Another sea creature, the swordfish, has a long snout shaped like a sword, but edged with tiny teeth. This large, powerful hunter catches its prey by swimming among a shoal of fish and slashing about wildly with its "sword". There have also been reports of swordfish piercing and sinking boats.

Do unicorns live in the sea?

Narwhals are small whales that swim in icy Arctic waters. Male narwhals have a strange left tooth that grows outwards from the gum to form a long, spiralling tusk. In times past, narwhals' tusks found on beaches were sold as precious unicorn horns.

Are mermaids real?

IN BYGONE TIMES, SAILORS WHO HAD SPENT LONG MONTHS at sea sometimes reported seeing mermaids – creatures with the head and body of a woman and a fish's tail. Experts now believe these stories may have been inspired by dugongs – rare sea mammals with rounded faces which hold their bodies upright in the water.

Female dugongs sometimes cuddle their babies in their front flippers while they suckle, another human-like trait.

Dugong

Hammerhead shark

The flattened shape of the hammerhead's "hammer" may also help it float and manoeuvre.

What has up to 3,000 teeth?

Hunting sharks have triangular teeth with serrated (jagged) edges like a saw. A shark may have as many as 3,000 teeth in its mouth, arranged in up to 20 rows, but only the teeth on the outer edge of the jaw are actually used for biting. The inner teeth move outwards to replace worn or broken teeth, so the shark's working set remain razor-sharp.

Are all sharks deadly?

No. Scientists have identified about 380 different kinds of shark. Relatively few species are fierce predators that hunt large prey such as seals, squid and penguins. Most sharks, such as whale sharks and basking sharks, feed on tiny creatures which they filter from the water using their sieve-like mouths. No harm will come to you if you meet one – unless you die of fright!

Which shark has a head like a hammer?

THE HAMMERHEAD SHARK IS NAMED FOR ITS CURIOUS HEAD, SHAPED like a giant letter "T". The shark's eyes and nostrils are set on the ends of its "hammer". As it moves along the sea-bed, it swings its head from side to side. Some scientists believe that the widely spaced eyes and nostrils help the hammerhead to home in on its prey.

The great white shark is nicknamed "white death". Its scientific name means "jagged teeth".

How do sharks track down their prey?

SHARKS HAVE MANY SENSES THAT HELP WITH HUNTING. AN excellent sense of smell allows the shark to detect tiny amounts of blood dissolved in the water, and track down distant wounded animals. A special sense called "distant touch" helps it to pick up vibrations caused by swimming creatures. At closer range, sensory pores on the shark's snout detect tiny electrical signals given off by prey animals' muscles. Sight and hearing also help the shark as it moves in for the kill.

What would sink if it didn't swim?

Most fish have a special organ called a swim bladder that helps them to float. Sharks have no swim bladder, so they must keep swimming to avoid sinking. Moving forward also keeps a supply of oxygen-rich sea-water flowing over the shark's gills, which helps it breathe.

What makes one shark bite another?

The smell of blood sometimes excites sharks so much they go into a "feeding frenzy". A group of feeding sharks will start to snap wildly and bite one another, and may even tear one of their number to pieces in the excitement.

Great white shark

What is the world's most deadly shark?

The great white shark is the world's most feared sea creature. It is responsible for more attacks on humans than any other shark. Great whites grow to 7 m (23 feet) long. Their jaws are so powerful they can sever a human arm or leg in a single bite. Tiger and mako sharks are also known as killers.

What creature holds the record for long-distance ocean travel?
Grey whales are the champion travellers of the oceans. Each year, they journey from their breeding grounds in the tropics to feeding grounds in the Arctic, and back again – a round trip of up to 20,000 km (12,500 miles).

Grey whale

Grey whales swim such huge distances on migration that scientists use satellites to track them.

Can dolphins talk?
Dolphins make all sorts of noises, from clicks and squeals to groans and whistles. A school of hunting dolphins keep in constant touch with one another through these noises, and "talk" together to co-ordinate their hunt.

Each dolphin has its own special whistle which helps the other members of its school to pinpoint its position during a hunt.

Why do whales and dolphins come to the surface?

WHALES AND DOLPHINS LOOK A LOT LIKE FISH, BUT THEY ARE REALLY sea-going mammals. Like all mammals, they breathe oxygen from the air, and so must surface to breathe. One or two nostrils called blowholes on top of the animal's head allow it to breathe without lifting its head from the water. But dolphins and some whales sometimes rear right out of the water to look around, a technique called spy-hopping.

Dolphins

What hunts by sonar?

Dolphins hunt with the aid of their own built-in sonar system, called echolocation. As they swim along, they produce a stream of clicking sounds. Sound waves from the clicks spread out through the water. When they hit an object, such as a shoal of fish, they bounce back. The dolphin can sense the size and movements of its prey by listening to the echoes.

What sleeps in a duvet of seaweed?

The sea otter makes its home among the kelp weed beds of the eastern Pacific. While resting, the otter wraps seaweed fronds around its body so it does not drift away with the ocean currents.

What eats its lunch in a bubble?

Humpback whales feed on small fish and krill floating near the sea surface. Sometimes they use a technique called bubble-netting to catch their prey. The whale lurks below a shoal of fish, then swims slowly upwards, blowing a stream of bubbles. The fish are trapped inside the net of bubbles and cannot escape from the whale's open jaws.

Which is the friendliest sea creature?

Dolphins are naturally playful and friendly to humans. They often swim alongside boats, riding on the bow-wave. Dolphins called "friendlies" regularly visit tourist beaches to swim with holiday-makers. There are many reports of dolphins rescuing drowning people, and even saving swimmers from sharks.

The sea otter is a skillful tool-user

Which is the cleverest sea creature?

DOLPHINS ARE AMONG THE WORLD'S MOST intelligent creatures. Tests in aquariums show they learn to perform new tasks quickly, and can even pass on their skills by "talking" to dolphins in other tanks. Sea otters are clever too, for they are one of the few animals able to use tools. The otter feeds on sea urchins, crabs and other shelled creatures. It breaks open the shells by smashing them against a flat rock balanced on its chest.

Sea otter

Which sea creature feeds on its mate's blood?

Deep-sea anglerfish have unusual sex lives. The females are up to 20 times bigger than the males! When a tiny male meets a female, he clamps on to her side with his powerful jaws and won't let go. Eventually he becomes fused to her body and feeds on her blood. The female has a handy supply of sperm to fertilize her eggs – but has to carry the "hanger-on" wherever she goes.

Which creature has a midwife at the birth?

Pregnant dolphins give birth to a single baby up to a year after mating. Experienced female dolphins known as "midwives" help at the birth. They may support the mother's body or help lift the baby to the surface so it can breathe.

What makes a fiddler crab sexy?

Male fiddler crabs have a built-in "sex symbol" – one claw that is much bigger than the other. On the sea-shore, the males attract attention by scuttling up and down waving their giant claws. The females choose the most energetic males with the biggest claws to mate with.

How do humpback whales go courting?

Humpback whales make many different sounds, including clicks, squeaks, moans and roars. To attract a partner, the male humpback sings a "song" made up of different noises. Each male sings a different tune, lasting for hours or even days. Humans enjoy the whale-song too – recordings of humpbacks have been made into hit CDs.

How do deep-sea creatures light up each others' lives?

In the darkness of the deep sea, many fish use light to attract a mate. Deep-sea viperfish and dragonfish have lines of tiny lights running along their bellies. Males and females have different patterns of lights, and can recognize the opposite sex when they see the right pattern.

The fiddler crab's giant claw gives him sex appeal, but is little help when feeding.

Fiddler crab

How do octopuses show their feelings?

Octopus and squid can change their skin colour from brown to green or blue. They use this skill to camouflage themselves when hunting, but also change colour to express emotions such as anger, and to attract a mate.

How does the damsel fish look after its eggs?

Most fish take little care of their eggs – they just spawn (lay and fertilize their eggs) and swim away without a backward glance. Some kinds of damsel fish are different. The females glue their eggs carefully to rocks. The males are caring fathers. They guard and check the eggs until they hatch, and shoo off any other fish that approach to eat them.

Which male fish gets pregnant?

Sea-horses have extraordinary breeding habits. The female lays her eggs in a little pouch on the male sea-horse's belly. The eggs develop in the safety of the pouch. About a month later, an amazing sight occurs, as the male "gives birth" to hundreds of tiny sea-horses.

Green turtles

Green turtles swim hundreds of kilometres to lay their eggs on the beach where they hatched out.

What sea creature comes ashore to breed?

GREEN TURTLES SPEND THEIR WHOLE LIVES AT SEA, but come on land to breed. The female swims ashore and clambers up the beach. Then she digs a deep hole and lays her eggs. When the baby turtles hatch they dig themselves out of the sand, then dash down to the waves and swim away quickly.

Blue whales

A blue whale calf drinks 100 litres (175 pints) of its mother's milk a day.

Which creature has the world's largest baby?

FEMALE BLUE WHALES, THE LARGEST WHALES, ALSO BEAR THE biggest babies. A newborn blue whale calf measures 7 m (23 feet) long and may weigh 2.5 tonnes – as much as a full-grown elephant! The thirsty baby drinks huge quantities of its mother's milk and puts on weight fast. At six months old, it may be as much as 16 m (54 feet) long.

What glues its eggs to the roof of its cave?
Female octopuses breed only once in their lifetime. After mating, the female lays long strings of eggs and glues them to the roof of her cave. She tends her eggs for up to six weeks, and never leaves her lair to go hunting. Many females die of hunger or exhaustion before their eggs hatch out.

What fish swims a long way to breed?
Young salmon hatch out and grow in shallow streams inland. After several years, they swim downriver to the sea and spend their adult lives in the ocean. To breed, they swim back and fight their way upriver, to spawn in the same stream where they hatched out.

What creature's birth was a mystery for centuries?
Eels were once a common sight in European streams and rivers. But their breeding habits were a mystery, for the eggs and baby eels were never seen. Then in the 1920s, experts at last discovered that the eels swim downriver and make their way across the Atlantic to breed. They spawn in the warm waters of the Sargasso Sea off the coast of Florida. When the eggs hatch out, the young eels drift slowly back to Europe and swim upriver.

How do young sea otters learn their skills?
Otters are naturally playful creatures. Young sea otters chase each other through the waving seaweeds and turn somersaults in the water. Mother otters sometimes bring their young an injured fish to play with. As the pups take turns to catch their weakened prey, they learn hunting skills that will be vital when they are older.

Sea catfish

Which young fish eats its brothers and sisters?

Sand tiger shark eggs hatch out inside their mother's body. The tiny embryo sharks feed on one another until only one big, strong baby is left, ready to be born.

How does the dugong protect its baby?

Female dugongs give birth to a single calf a year after mating. A close bond forms between mother and baby. As the female and her calf swim through the murky sea-grass, she calls out constantly, to make sure her baby is safe.

Which sea father has a mouthful of babies?

FEW FISH LOOK AFTER THEIR BABIES, BUT FISH known as mouthbrooders are the exception. Mouthbrooders such as sea catfish protect their young by hiding them in their mouths! In sea catfish, the male is the caring parent. The babies swim in a cloud near their dad's head. When danger threatens they scoot back inside his mouth.

Young catfish swim close to their father's mouth so they can dash inside if danger approaches.